LIFE IN ANCIENT CIVILIZATIONS

The Chinese
LIFE IN CHINA'S GOLDEN AGE

by **Matt Doeden**

illustrated by **Samuel Hiti**

M Millbrook Press · Minneapolis

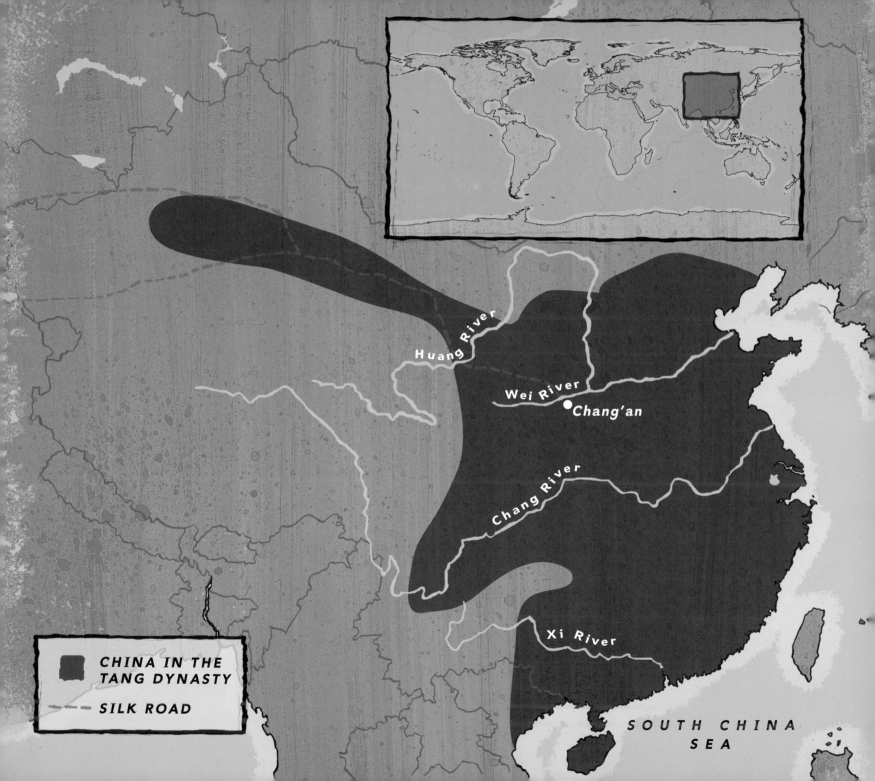

Huang River

Wei River

● Chang'an

Chang River

Xi River

SOUTH CHINA
SEA

CHINA IN THE
TANG DYNASTY

SILK ROAD

Introduction

China has a long and rich history. People have lived there for thousands of years. But the years from 618 to 907 stand out. This period is often called the Golden Age of China. It was mostly a peaceful time. In this era, China was known for its silk, inventions, and impressive temples.

Two dynasties, or ruling families, led the Chinese Empire during this time. They were the Tang dynasty and the Zhou dynasty. The city of Chang'an was the capital of the empire. Chang'an means "lasting peace." This city was home to artists, poets, and merchants. It was at the center of one of the world's great civilizations.

CHAPTER ONE

Living in Chang'an

Chang'an's busy streets were filled with people from many classes. The nobles were at the top. This class was made up of the emperor and his family. The nobles had power, money, and the best of everything.

Walls lined the main streets of Chang'an. They divided the city into areas called wards.

Other classes were below the nobles. Government workers helped
to run the empire. Thousands of religious leaders led the faiths of
China. Peasants farmed the land. They also did common labor. Craftsmen
and merchants sold their goods. A small number of slaves made up the
lowest class. They were often captured soldiers from other places.

The peasant class was by far the largest. Peasant farmers grew most of the food for China. All people ate grains such as rice, wheat, and millet. Fruits and vegetables were also part of many meals.

The Chinese ate several types of meat. Pork, fish, or lamb was often part of a meal. Bear and snake were rare treats. Some people even ate insects! Water was the most common drink. But the Chinese also loved to drink tea.

Farmers pedaled a machine to carry water from ditches and streams to crops on higher ground. Slats of wood pushed water up through the machine as the men pedaled.

Clothing was made from silk, felt, or hemp. Only nobles and government workers were allowed to wear silk. Different levels of officials wore different colors of silk.

Men wore loose pants and a shirt that fastened in front. They tied a sash around the waist. They often wore cloth caps. Women wore a floor-length skirt with a shirt or coat. They wore hairpins and combs in their hair. In cold weather, people kept warm under sheepskins or animal furs.

Women wore jewelry such as earrings, bracelets, and necklaces. The finest jewelry was made with pearls or jade. Noblemen sometimes wore pendants and belts decorated with jade.

Detailed designs were carved into jade jewelry. This jade pendant shows a monkey playing in grape vines.

Women of the noble class enjoyed relaxed lives. Their Pekingese dogs did too. Only the highest classes could own this breed.

Children lived a strict life. They were taught to respect adults. They learned skills such as farming or trading from their parents. Few people went to school. Most couldn't read or write. But children of the nobles attended schools or learned from tutors.

For boys, childhood lasted until the age of nineteen. Then they were "capped" and became men. Fathers placed cloth caps on their sons' heads. The sons were also given new, adult names. Girls had a similar ceremony around the age of fourteen. Mothers pinned up their daughters' hair to show that they were ready for marriage.

More boys than girls went to school. They studied poetry, history, mathematics, religion, and more.

Most girls learned how to spin
thread and cook at home.

CHAPTER TWO

Chinese Beliefs

Not all Chinese followed one religion. Three main faiths were part of the Golden Age. Buddhism was the most common. It had come to China from India almost six hundred years before the Tang dynasty began.

Buddhism focuses on the relationship between people and nature. It includes many gods and natural spirits. Chinese Buddhists believed that spirits lived in objects. These included rocks, trees, houses, and mountains. Buddhists tried to please these spirits. They also believed in reincarnation. Souls returned to life again and again. Good deeds were rewarded by blessings in the next life. Bad deeds were punished.

A man known as the Buddha started the Buddhist religion. This Chinese statue of him is from the Golden Age.

Many religious men and women lived in Buddhist monasteries. These centers of study and worship were popular during the Golden Age.

Taoism is a belief system that grew out of some of China's oldest faiths. Taoists believe nature has opposite forces. They are called yin and yang. Yin is dark, heavy, and wet. Yang is light, airy, and dry. They can stand for other opposites too. The balance of yin and yang is always changing. This causes changes in health, nature, and even the stars. So balance in life is important to Taoists. Over time, Taoists adopted some Buddhist beliefs. Gods became a part of Taoism.

Some Taoists tried to live forever. They did exercises, ate certain foods, practiced breathing, and prayed.

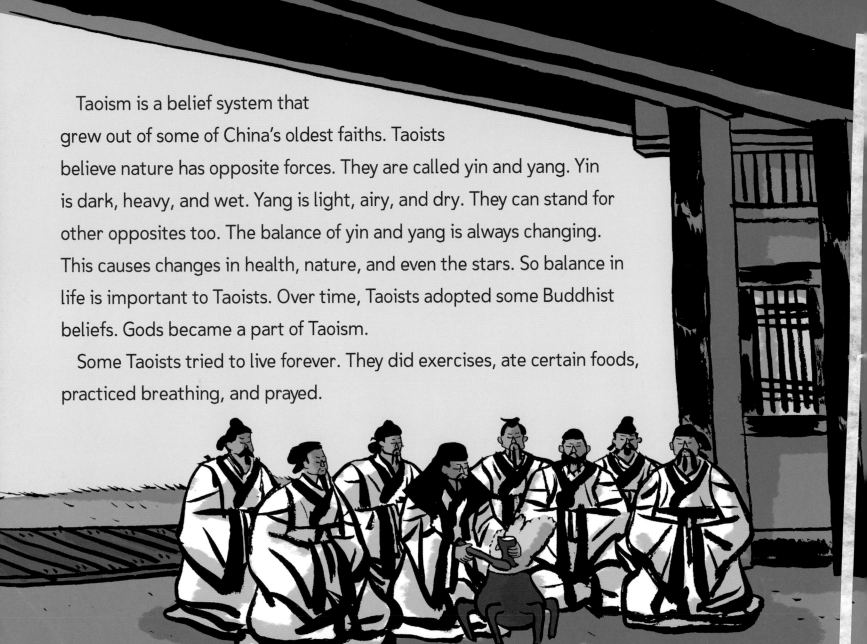

The yin-yang symbol (*left*) shows how yin and yang work together in nature. The two forces are always in motion. They are opposite but are also part of each other.

Confucianism had been popular in China since the 400s B.C. It didn't include gods and spirits. Instead, it offered a way to a better society. By the Golden Age, it was less important than it had been in the past. But it was still a part of the culture.

Confucianism focuses on rules and guidelines for moral behavior. A Buddhist or Taoist person could still follow Confucian rules in life.

In about the 700s, the religions Christianity and Islam also arrived in China. Each gained a small but loyal following.

Confucianism is based on the teachings of Confucius. (He is also called Kongzi.) He lived from 551 to 479 B.C.

The ancient Chinese celebrated almost thirty holidays. The Last Day of the Twelfth Moon was one holiday. It took place just before the New Year. Families placed images of a god above their stoves at the beginning of each year. They believed that the god watched the house and recorded the family's sins. At the end of the year, it left Earth to report the sins.

On the Last Day of the Twelfth Moon, families offered fruit or honey to the image of the god. They hoped that these offerings would get them a good report!

Fireworks light up the sky over the city of Hong Kong as part of a modern Chinese New Year celebration.

During the Tang dynasty, the Chinese learned how to make fireworks. They set them off as the New Year approached. They believed the fire and loud sounds would scare away evil spirits.

21

CHAPTER THREE

Homes and Temples

Chang'an was a large, busy city. A wall 18 feet (5 meters) tall surrounded it. Inside the wall were marketplaces, parks, temples, and homes. Many people had small homes. A few lived in mansions.

Few buildings of the Golden Age survived to modern times. That was because the Chinese built with mainly wood and bamboo. These materials didn't last long. Buildings were always being remade. Stone buildings can last much longer. But the Chinese didn't like building with stone. Stone buildings fall apart in earthquakes, which are common in China.

The famous Great Wall of China was built mostly before the Golden Age. Emperors had it built to protect the Chinese Empire from its enemies to the north.

The Chinese built outer walls around large homes. They packed earth tightly together to form the walls.

23

Mansions were large and fancy. Many were two stories tall. Small buildings and courtyards surrounded mansions. Nobles and high government officials enjoyed living in these homes.

Common homes were smaller and simpler. They had just one room. The roofs were covered in thatch. When possible, people built their homes facing south. They received the most sun that way.

A mansion's courtyard often
included a small lake. It may have
also had a garden of bamboo and
peonies, a favorite flower.

Chang'an had many impressive religious buildings. Temples called pagodas towered over the city. So did monasteries. One Buddhist monastery had a hall that stood 150 feet (46 m) tall!

Chang'an's most famous building was the Giant Wild Goose Pagoda. It was also known as the Large Goose Pagoda. This brick temple had eight stories. It stood 210 feet (64 m) tall. It represented a holy mountain. A similar temple called the Small Goose Pagoda was also built of brick. These are the only two buildings from this period that have survived into modern times.

Construction of the Large Goose Pagoda (*right*) began in 652. Work on the Small Goose Pagoda began in 707.

Building a pagoda took many men and several years to complete.

CHAPTER FOUR

Ideas and Inventions

During the Tang dynasty, China was a place of discovery and new ideas. It was filled with scientists and inventors.

Writing, paper, and print are among China's greatest inventions. Chinese people write with picturelike symbols. They began using them more than three thousand years ago. The writing has changed a lot over the years. More than four thousand symbols are used. These are called characters. Many modern characters were also in use during the Golden Age.

The first printed works were being made in China by the 800s. Characters were carved into a wood block. The block was pressed onto paper like a rubber stamp.

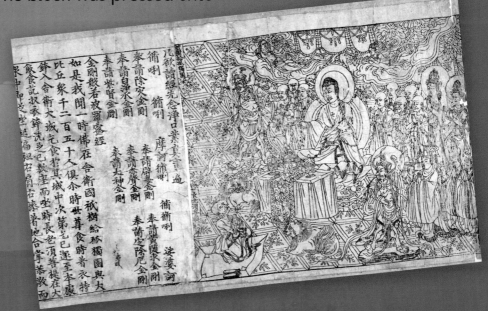

This book is called the Diamond Sutra. It is the oldest printed book that still exists. It was printed with wood blocks in 868.

Calligraphy (artistic writing) was one of the prized arts in Tang China. The numbers 1 through 10 (above) show some of the brushstrokes used in Chinese calligraphy.

In the Golden Age, China was known for silk fabric decorated with beautiful designs and paintings. To make the silk, the Chinese raised silkworms and collected the cocoons they spun. Next they unwound the cocoons. Finally they wove the tiny threads into cloth.

The fine fabric impressed visitors. Merchants brought goods from other parts of the world and traded them for silk. They also took new Chinese inventions back to their own lands. The main paths they traveled on became known as the Silk Road.

Silkworms eat leaves from the mulberry tree.

The city of Chang'an was located along the Silk Road.

The Chinese knew a lot about math and science. They invented a counting device called an abacus. They came up with the decimal system to count parts of a whole. They also studied the night sky and tracked the movements of planets.

During the Golden Age, Chinese scientists discovered gunpowder. They used it in fireworks and in weapons.

The list of Chinese inventions goes on and on. They created the magnetic compass, the kite, and the wheelbarrow. They built complex systems to water their crops. In later years, they even came up with the idea for paper money!

People in China's Golden Age used an abacus to help them count.

The Chinese enjoyed flying kites made of bamboo and paper.

CHAPTER FIVE

Famous People

China's Golden Age lasted almost three hundred years. A number of leaders left their mark on China during this time.

Two important rulers were Gaozu and his son, Taizong (*right*). Gaozu started the Tang dynasty in 618. Taizong took power eight years later. Taizong worked hard to make better laws for the empire. He set up a system of tests for government workers. The tests were a fair way for new officials to be selected. Taizong is remembered as one of the greatest emperors in Chinese history.

Gaozu was known as Li Yuan before he became emperor. Taizong (*pictured*) was called Li Shimin. In Chinese, a person's family name comes before the first name.

The Chinese system was not set up for women to rule. But in 683, something surprising happened. A woman named Empress Wu became the leader of the empire. She had ruled with her husband, the emperor. Then the emperor died. So Wu arranged for her youngest son to be emperor. But the boy was young, so she ruled in his place. In 690, she made herself empress. She began the Zhou dynasty.

Empress Wu, however, had many enemies. They made her give up the throne in 705. The Tang dynasty continued after her.

Empress Wu Zetian (right) was known for her beauty and her smart leadership.

Empress Wu chose talented people to do important jobs. China prospered while she was in power. However, people who disagreed with her were often killed.

Xuanzong was one of China's greatest emperors. He led for forty-four years. His rule began in 712 and was the true Golden Age.

Xuanzong was wise and fair. He stored up grain for times with less food. He supported the arts. He improved health care and education in his empire. He did away with the death penalty. His reign was a time of great peace and prosperity for the Chinese.

Xuanzong was also called Minghuang, or "brilliant emperor." He enjoyed music and theater.

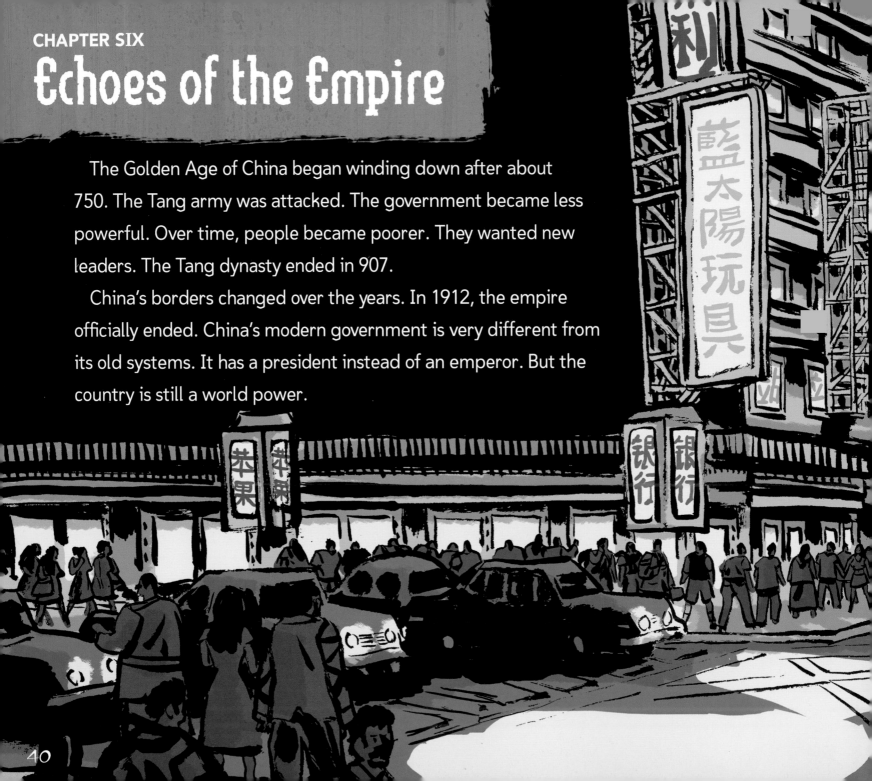

CHAPTER SIX
Echoes of the Empire

The Golden Age of China began winding down after about 750. The Tang army was attacked. The government became less powerful. Over time, people became poorer. They wanted new leaders. The Tang dynasty ended in 907.

China's borders changed over the years. In 1912, the empire officially ended. China's modern government is very different from its old systems. It has a president instead of an emperor. But the country is still a world power.

More people live in modern China than in any other country.
It has a population of more than one billion people.

The culture of China's people has changed a lot. But many things, from religion to traditional foods to clothing, have remained. Its people are proud of its long, rich past.

The city of Chang'an still exists. It was renamed Xi'an in the 1300s. It is home to more than three million people. In the modern city, you can still see the Large Goose and Small Goose pagodas. A newer, taller city wall surrounds Xi'an. The wall stands as a reminder of the Tang dynasty. The Golden Age may be gone, but it is not forgotten.

Islam has become one of the major religions of Xi'an. Its Great Mosque (right) is one of the modern city's best-known buildings.

Xi'an's city wall was rebuilt in the 1370s. It is the most complete city wall still standing in China.

TIMELINE

617   Li Yuan leads a rebellion (a fight) against China's Sui dynasty.

618   Li Yuan becomes Emperor Gaozu and begins the Tang dynasty. He rules his empire from the city of Chang'an.

683   Empress Wu rules the empire in place of her young son.

690   Empress Wu begins the Zhou dynasty.

705   The Tang dynasty continues after Empress Wu leaves power.

712   Xuanzong takes control of China. He reigns for forty-four years. That time includes the empire's true Golden Age.

756   A rebellion led by a foreigner named An Lushan ends the rule of Xuanzong.

763   War and rebellion begin to cause the government to lose control of much of its empire.

805   Emperor Xianzong takes control of China. He begins to regain central control of the empire.

907   The Tang dynasty ends.

1300s   Chang'an is renamed Xi'an.

PRONUNCIATION GUIDE

abacus: A-buh-kuhs

Buddhism: BOOD-ihzm

calligraphy: kuh-LIHG-ruh-fee

Chang'an: CHAHNG-AHN

Confucianism: kuhn-FYOO-shuhn-ihzm

dynasty: DY-nuh-stee

Gaozu: GOWD-zuh

Li Shimin: LEE SHUR-MIHN

Li Yuan: LEE yoo-AHN

Minghuang: MING-HWAHNG

pagoda: puh-GOH-duh

reincarnation: REE-ihn-car-NAY-shuhn

Taizong: TIED-ZUNG

Tang: TAHNG

Taoism: DOW-ihzm

Wu Zetian: WOO ZUH-tee-EHN

Xi'an: SHEE-AHN

Xuanzong: shoo-AHND-ZUNG

Zhou: JOH

GLOSSARY

ancient: very old

bamboo: a type of grass with a hollow, woody stem, often used for building in ancient China

Buddhism: a religion based on the relationship between people and nature

characters: symbols used in writing. Chinese characters stand for words or parts of a word.

Confucianism: a code of behavior created by the philosopher Confucius around 500 B.C.

dynasty: a ruling family. A dynasty may last through the rule of the family's parents, children, grandchildren, and more.

emperor: the leader of an empire

empire: a group of lands and people under the control of one powerful leader

gunpowder: an explosive chemical discovered around the 900s in China

jade: a gemstone that is usually green. Jade was treasured in China.

merchants: people who buy and sell goods to make a living

monastery: a place where monks and nuns (religious men and women) live and work

pagoda: a Buddhist temple

peasant: a member of a low-ranking, usually farming, class of society

Taoism: a religion that grew out of the local faiths of ancient China and nearby regions. It focused on balance in life and the structure of the afterlife.

thatch: a plant material, such as straw, used to cover a roof

FURTHER READING

Challen, Paul C. *Life in Ancient China*. New York: Crabtree Pub., 2005.
The author covers the development of ancient China, its religions, art, and daily life.

Major, John S. *The Silk Route: 7,000 Miles of History*. New York: HarperCollins, 1995.
With colorful illustrations, this book explores the Silk Road, the route merchants traveled to and from Chang'an.

Riehecky, Janet. *China*. Minneapolis: Lerner Publications Company, 2008.
Color photos and accessible text explore modern China's land, people, food, and culture.

Sheldon, Ken, ed. *If I Were a Kid in Ancient China*. Peterborough, NH: Cricket Books, 2006.
In a light tone, the author describes what life would be like for a child living during the Han dynasty of China.

Zemlicka, Shannon. *Colors of China*. Minneapolis: Millbrook Press, 2002.
Simple text and bright, full-page illustrations introduce China through the colors that are found in Chinese life and history.

WEBSITES

The British Museum—Ancient China
http://www.ancientchina.co.uk/menu.html
The British Museum's site on ancient China includes a history on the formation of China, a detailed explanation of its writing system, and more.

China, 500–1000 A.D.
http://www.metmuseum.org/TOAH/ht/06/eac/ht06eac.htm
The Metropolitan Museum of Art's website gives a detailed timeline of Chinese history, with a focus on the happenings during the Tang dynasty.

China Travel—Giant Wild Goose Pagoda
http://www.china-travel-golden-route.com/goose_pagoda.html
This site on tourist attractions in China features the Giant Wild Goose Pagoda, with photographs and detailed descriptions of what awaits visitors inside.

INDEX

PHOTO ACKNOWLEDGMENTS

The images in this book are used with the permission of: © Bill Hauser/Independent Picture Service, p. 4;
© Werner Forman/Art Resource, NY, pp. 10, 14; © Richard A. Brooks/The Image Bank/Getty Images,
p. 20; © Digital Vision/Getty Images, p. 22; © Eddie Gerald/Alamy, p. 26; © British Library/HIP/The Image
Works, p. 28; © Inga Spence/Visuals Unlimited, Inc., p. 30; © Keren Su/China Span/Alamy, p. 32; The Art
Archive/British Library, p. 36; © Marco Secchi/Alamy, p. 42.

About the Illustrations
Samuel Hiti, who has a background in comic-book art, rendered the illustrations for the Life in Ancient Civilizations series using brush, ink, and computer. Hiti researched each civilization to develop distinct color palettes for these books and create his interpretations of life in these cultures.

The publisher wishes to thank Professor Ann Waltner, University of Minnesota Department of History, for serving as a consultant on this title.

Millbrook Press
A division of Lerner Publishing Group, Inc.
241 First Avenue North
Minneapolis, MN 55401 U.S.A.

Website address: www.lernerbooks.com

Library of Congress Cataloging-in-Publication Data

Doeden, Matt.
    The Chinese : life in China's golden age / by Matt Doeden ; illustrated by Samuel Hiti.
        p.   cm. — (Life in ancient civilizations)
    Includes index.
    ISBN: 978–0–8225–8681–4 (lib. bdg. : alk. paper)
    1. China—Civilization—221 B.C.–A.D. 960—Juvenile literature. I. Hiti, Samuel. II. Title.
DS749.35.D64 2010
951'.01—dc22   2008048885

Manufactured in the United States of America
1 2 3 4 5 6 – DP – 15 14 13 12 11 10